Wait a minute... I'll get you my recipe

A personal collection from the Kitchen of Carol Brandon Bergeron

The Berkshire Traveller Press
Stockbridge, Massachusetts
01262

Second Printing

Bergeron, Carol Brandon.
Wait a minute ... I'll get you my recipe.

1. Cookery.   I. Title.
TX715.B4828   641.5   74-11508
ISBN 0-912944-24-2

© 1974 Berkshire Traveller Press

This is a personal collection geared, I hope, to your way of doing things — of recipes — from many sources, including "the top of my head" — and of other things I've learned that may be of help in the kitchen and elsewhere.

"We may live without poetry, music
    and art;
We may live without conscience and
    live without heart;
We may live without friends, we may
    live without books;
But civilized man cannot live
    without cooks.

He may live without books, — what is
    knowledge but grieving?
He may live without hope, — what is
    hope but deceiving?
He may live without love, — what is
    passion but pining?
But where is the man that can
    live without dining?"
                    Owen Meredith

From the kitchen of Carol Brandon Bergeron.

Table of Contents

Chives

Chicken

Fish

Cheese and Other Good Things

Desserts

Herbs

"Lavender blue,
dilly dilly,
Rosemary green."

Mother Goose

Herbs

Just a pinch of this or that herb makes all the difference.

Basic Ten Herbs for the shelf:

1. Basil - tomatoes, meats, cheeses, soups
2. Dill - pickles, salads, potatoes, breads
3. Marjoram - meats, soups, salads, vegetables
4. Mint - meats, salads, beverages
5. Oregano - tomatoes, pasta dishes
6. Parsley - anything
7. Rosemary - chicken, lamb, pork, fish, turnips
8. Sage - cheese, pork, stuffings poultry
9. Savory - meats, vegetables
10. Thyme - soups, poultry, salads, stuffing

Herb Mixtures:

Soup: Bay, thyme, savory

Chicken: 1. Parsley, marjoram
2. Marjoram, savory, basil
3. Basil, thyme

Cream Sauce: Basil, marjoram, thyme

Ground Beef: Basil, thyme, parsley

Lamb or Veal: Marjoram, rosemary, savory

Herb Sauces

Mint

Melt a small jar of red currant jelly, then stir in 2T finely minced fresh mint leaves (or dried mint freshened in a few drops of orange juice), add 1T grated orange rind. Good with lamb or ham.

For a quick & flavorful tomato sauce cook half a cup each chopped onion and green pepper in 2T olive oil until soft. Sprinkle with 1/2 t dried basil and add 1 can tomato sauce. Simmer 15 minutes.

Vinaigrette

8 T olive oil
5 T herb vinegar
1 medium dill pickle chopped
1/4 t each salt and pepper
1 mashed hard-boiled egg yolk
1 t each chervil, chives, tarragon
    and basil

Mix and beat thoroughly.

Herb Cheeses

½ lb. strong cheddar cheese grated
4 T heavy cream
3 T sweet sherry
2 T butter
2 T mixed finely chopped sage, parsley,
    chives, thyme and chervil
Salt to taste

Mash cheese and other ingredients with
a fork until well mixed.
Place over simmering water in double
boiler and heat until creamy and
pale green in color.
Pour in small pots and cool before
using.   Yield two cups.

An old English recipe and a lovely
Christmas gift.

Sage

A simpler one: to ½ lb. strong cheddar
grated into a bowl, add ½ c red
burgundy and 1 t crumbled dried
sage leaves, mix well, let stand
at room temperature to blend
for an hour or two.

Herb Butters

To ½ c soft butter add and cream well:

For Lamb –
    1 clove garlic, minced
    1 t rosemary
    dash of lemon juice

For Chicken – spread on before broiling or roasting
    1 t parsley
    ⅛ t tarragon

For Fish –
    1 t parsley
    ½ t marjoram
    garnish with sliced olives

For Bread –
    ⅛ t garlic salt
    ½ t each thyme, marjoram, rosemary

For Canapé spread –
    ½ t oregano
    1 T parsley
    ½ t poppy seed

If any is left over it will keep well in a covered jar in the refrigerator.

Remoulade

A cold sauce, highly spiced, and usually served with cold fish or meat. We haven't had shrimp with cocktail sauce since my husband had Shrimp Remoulade at Arnaud's in New Orleans. He says this is close.

1½ c mayonnaise
1 T dijon style mustard
1 T finely chopped sweet gherkins
1 t finely chopped capers
1 t each parsley, chives, tarragon and chervil
Anchovy paste the size of a hazelnut

Add all to mayonnaise and mix (I use the blender). Taste for salt — it depends on your mayonnaise — and you may want to add more mustard.

This really does things for cold ham or tongue.

Keeps well, refrigerated.

Don't try it on a humid day!

Fluffy Mustard Sauce

This is a variation on my mother's recipe.
I discovered it makes a beautiful
salad dressing when mixed with
the juice from stuffed olives.

3 egg yolks	2 T water
1/4 c dry mustard	2 T butter
2 T sugar	2 T prepared horseradish
1 1/2 t salt	1 1/2 c cream for
1/4 c cider vinegar	whipping

Beat yolks in the top of a double boiler,
blend in vinegar, mustard, sugar, salt
and water. Cook, stirring constantly
over simmering water 5 minutes or until
thickened. Remove from heat. Stir in
butter until melted, add horseradish.
Cool _completely_, then beat until fluffy.

Beat cream until stiff, fold in mustard
mixture. Chill.

Pack this in small jars. It makes
a lovely gift when you attach a
card with serving suggestions —
   e.g. cold meats, hard cooked eggs, etc.

Keeps well, refrigerated.

Season Salt

Try it on salads — and on potatoes.

1 C coarse salt*
1 t each thyme, garlic salt and
    curry powder
1/2 t onion powder
1/4 t dill seed
1 1/2 t oregano
2 1/2 t paprika
2 t dry mustard

If you have a mortar and pestle, fine.
If not use a small wooden bowl and
the back of a wooden spoon to crush
the herbs with the salt.

*You can buy kosher salt in most
supermarkets — in about three
pound boxes. It is marvelous for
salads — doesn't wilt the greens —
and looks elegant in a small dish
on the table.

It is traditional with us that
salt, which is a symbol of hospitality,
is always the first thing put on the
table, and the last removed.

16

Substitutions

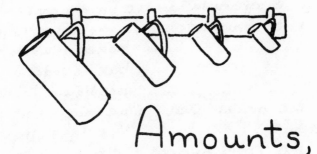

Amounts, Equivalents

"Enough's
as good as a feast."
George Chapman

Substitutions

Sugar:

1 c granulated	1 c firmly packed brown
1 c granulated	1 c molasses, syrup or honey plus ¼ to ½ t baking soda and ¼ c less liquid in recipe
1 c granulated	1½ c maple syrup and ¼ c less liquid
1 c corn syrup	1 c granulated plus ¼ c liquid (do not substitute for more than ½ of syrup)
1 c honey	1 c sugar plus ¼ c liquid
½ c honey	½ c sugar

Flour:

1 c pastry flour	1 c all-purpose flour less 2T
1 T cornstarch	2 T flour (as thickening)
1 t baking powder	¼ t baking soda plus ½ t cream of tartar

1 square chocolate	3T unsweetened cocoa plus 1t shortening

Shortening:
1 c butter	7/8·1c hydrogenated fat
1 c butter	7/8 c lard
1 c butter	1 c margarine
oils	do not substitute

Milk and Cream:
1 c fresh milk	1/2 c evaporated milk plus 1/2 c water
1 c fresh milk	1/2c condensed milk plus 1/2 c water (reduce sugar in recipe)
1 c fresh milk	4T powdered whole milk plus 1C water
1 c fresh milk	4T powdered skim milk plus 2T butter plus 1 c water
1 c cream (light)	7/8 c milk plus 3 T butter
1 c cream (heavy)	3/4 c milk plus 1/3 c butter
1 c buttermilk	1 c sweet milk plus 1 T lemon juice or vinegar, let it stand 10 minutes

Amounts

When the recipe calls for: You need

Bread: 1 c soft crumbs   2 slices
       1 c small cubes   2 slices
       2 c stuffing mix   ½ 8oz. package

Cereal: 1 c crushed flakes   3 c
       2 c cooked cornmeal   ½ c

Pasta-Rice: 4c cooked spaghetti   8oz. package
       2 c cooked elbows   1 c uncooked
       3½c cooked noodles   8oz. package
       4 c cooked rice   1 c raw

Dairy: 8T butter or margarine   1 stick = ¼ lb.
       2 c butter   1 lb.
       2 c cottage cheese   1 lb.
       1 c grated cheese   ¼ lb.
       1 c whipped cream   ½ c whipping cream
       ⅔ c evaporated milk   1 small can

Meat: 3 c diced cooked meat   1 lb. cooked
       2 c ground cooked meat   1 lb. cooked
       4 c diced cooked chicken   5 lb. hen

Fish:

¾ c crab meat	6½ oz. can
1 c lobster meat	6½ oz. can
25 shrimp	4½ oz. can

Fruit:

4 c sliced apples	4 medium
2 c sliced strawberries	1 pint
4 c sliced peaches	2 lbs. or 8 medium
1 c orange juice	3 medium
1 c mashed banana	3 medium

Sugar:

2⅓ c granulated	1 lb.
4-4½ c 10x (confectioner's powdered)	1 lb.
2¼ c brown-packed	1 lb.
120 pieces loaf sugar	1 lb.

Fresh Vegetables:

4 c sliced raw potato	4 medium
4 c diced cooked green beans	1 lb.
1 c shelled peas	1 lb.
1 c chopped onion	1 large
2½ c cooked fresh tomatoes	4 medium = 1 lb.
1 c grated raw carrot	1 large

When the recipe calls for: you need

Nuts:

1 c walnuts	½ lb. in shell	2oz. shelled
1 c almonds	½ lb. in shell	2½oz. shelled
1 c pecans	½ lb. in shell	1½oz. shelled
1 c peanuts	½ lb. in shell	3½oz. shelled
1 c filberts	¾ lb. in shell	2oz. shelled

Equivalents

Flavoring and Extract Equivalents

Banana	½ t	=	½ c bananas
Cherry	½ t	=	½ c cherries
Lemon or Lime	1½ t	=	1 lemon or lime
Orange	1 t	=	1 medium orange
Rum	1 T	=	⅓ c rum
Brandy	1 T	=	⅓ c brandy
Raspberry	½ t	=	½ c berries
Strawberry	½ t	=	¼ c berries

... And - don't forget...
"A pint's a pound
the world around".

Have You Ever Thought Of...

"Thought makes everything
fit for use."
R.W. Emerson

Have you ever thought of...

running your finger around the inside of the shell halves when cracking eggs? On a dozen eggs, what adheres amounts to about one extra white.

adding a good pinch of salt to very sour fruit (such as apples) when cooking them? You will need much less sugar to sweeten them.

using the last piece of pie from dinner for a great treat at breakfast?

putting seasoned ground beef (no liquid please) in a buttered pyrex pie plate — dotting with butter and broiling it like steak?

grating together raw Idaho potato and an onion, and dropping mixture by spoonfuls into hot sizzling butter in a fry pan for lace potato cakes?

chilling cheese to grate it more easily?

storing egg whites against the day you make a soufflé or meringue? They keep 3-4 days refrigerated.

stretching crab or lobster for salad by adding small cubes of bread trimmed of crust? Marinated with seafood for an hour, the bread swells and picks up flavor of fish and dressing.

melting a square or two of chocolate in a soup ladle? It is simpler to handle than a hot cup or bowl — and it pours.

lightly sautéeing small bits of salami or prosciutto and adding to peas or green beans?

keeping a small jar in the freezer to collect dried scraps of cheese (cheddar, cheshire, swiss or parmesan)? Grate in blender for casserole toppings or to add to sauces.

Have you ever thought of...

substituting plain yogurt for sour cream? Fewer calories and more nutritious.

adding a dash of nutmeg to mashed potatoes — especially the instant variety? It makes them taste more "potatoey."

making your own paté by sautéeing chicken livers and onions together and putting them, with a hard-boiled egg or two, through a meat grinder or in a blender?

mixing a pound of hamburger with celery and onion salt and shaping six patties to freeze separately for quick breakfasts? Faster than eggs — and a great change.

strawberry shortcake for a summer breakfast? With biscuit mix in the refrigerator, it is a snap to do.

Meats

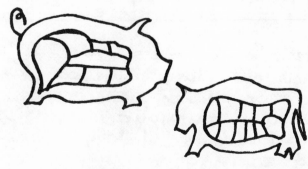

"The discovery
    of a new dish

does more for the
    happiness of man

than the discovery
    of a new star."

Brillat-Savarin

A Steak Rule of Thumb

1 inch steak should be cooked
   3 inches from heat.
2 inch steak should be cooked
   4 inches from heat.
3 inch steak should be cooked
   6 inches from heat.

Broil until one side is brown — broil until other side is brown — turning only once.

Let rest a few minutes on a warm plate before slicing. Thin steaks should be served immediately. A 1½ inch steak should be cooked 8 minutes on one side, 7 minutes on second side for rare. Add 1 minute per side for medium rare, another minute for medium. If you like it well done — you are on your own — I won't be a party to such desecration.

To test for doneness — make a small cut close to the bone and look — or better yet, press gently with your finger tips. It should be slightly resistant and springy.

Mother's Pot Roast

3-4 lb. rolled chuck
  or bottom round
3/4 c sour cream at
  room temperature
Salt and pepper
1 clove garlic
1 carrot diced
1 onion diced

3/4 c warmed red
  wine
3 T flour
1/2 c water
juice of 1/2 lemon

Rub the salt and pepper into the meat, and brown the roast in hot fat in a heavy pan with a close fitting lid. Add the vegetables and brown lightly. Add heated wine. Stir in the cream. Cover tightly and cook very slowly 2½ to 3 hours. Remove meat. Skim off fat. Add flour and water mixed. Cook about 5 minutes. Add lemon.

Serves 6.

This is even better the second day. Plan to serve it with noodles or potatoes — the gravy deserves them.

Boeuf Bourguignon David

2 lbs. lean stewing beef
(I use chuck) cut in
1 1/2 inch cubes
2 T butter divided
1 T oil
1 T flour
1 1/2 c red wine
1 t salt
1/4 t fresh ground
pepper
1/2 lb. small white
onions

1 carrot
1/2 lb. mushrooms
1 clove garlic
4 shallots
Bouquet Garni
(parsley, thyme, bay)
a veal knuckle or
beef bone
1/2 c light port or
medium sherry
1 oz. brandy

Get the oil and 1 T butter bubbling in a heavy pot and brown the meat until it is "closed." Remove the meat, add flour to the pot and brown well. Add the salt, pepper and red wine and stir until smooth. Return meat to the pot.

Slice the vegetables and in a separate pot brown 2/3 of your onions in the remaining butter. Add all of the vegetables to the meat with the Bouquet Garni, the bone and the wine. Add enough water to bring the liquid level with the meat. Cover and simmer* very gently 3 - 4 hours,

30

until the meat is tender. Half an hour before serving add the brandy.

Dry boiled rice is a good companion to this.

*But this is how I do it - I put the Bourguignon in a 300°-325° oven, check to make sure it is just simmering — and forget it for a couple of hours. About an hour and a quarter before serving, I butter a casserole and using converted rice, salt, and the amount of water specified on the box, put it in the oven with the meat. When the meat is done, the rice will be also—all in the oven — no fuss—all you need to leave your guests for is to toss a salad.

Allow at least an hour's preparation time, plus cooking. Serves 6.

A cold winter's night can be brightened in many ways, rarely more satisfyingly than this.

Nancy's Beef Stew

This is a classic always requested on our holidays in New Hampshire, and, I think, the best beef stew we have ever eaten.

2 lbs. beef chuck in 1½ inch cubes
2 T oil
1 T flour
1 t salt
½ t pepper
1 clove garlic minced
1 large onion chopped
1 beef bouillon cube dissolved in 1 c hot water
1 8oz. can tomato sauce

9 peppercorns
2 whole cloves
¼ c chopped parsley
1 bay leaf
½ c sherry or dry vermouth
6 medium potatoes quartered
6 medium carrots in ½ inch slices
1 stalk celery sliced

Brown meat in oil. Be sure the meat is dry and the pan <u>hot</u> when you start so it browns quickly. When meat is "closed," sprinkle with flour seasoned with salt and pepper and brown again. While all this is going on, combine the garlic, onion, bouillon, tomato sauce, spices and herbs in a small pan and heat to boiling. Pour this over the meat, stir in and cover tightly. Simmer (I use my electric fry pan at 175°-200°) about 2 hours. Add wine and cook another ½ hour.

It can be refrigerated or frozen at this point.

About 3/4 hour before you want to serve, cook the potatoes, carrots and celery separately until nearly tender. While these cook, warm the meat and gravy if it has been refrigerated. Add the vegetables for the last 15 minutes of cooking. (At this point I often add a handful of frozen corn or peas.)

The meat is really better if cooked the day before — and adding the vegetables the last 15 minutes gives you great control of the situation when you are entertaining.

This is marvelous with a green salad— hot biscuits — and for dessert — fruit and cheese.

Serves 6.

Basic Spaghetti Sauce

This sauce was "developed" one summer on Cape Cod, when I was cooking for five of us on a two burner hot plate. We even managed Lasagne, with this as a base, by adding a top of burner oven — AND it was good!

1 lb. Italian sweet sausage or ground beef, or both
1 clove garlic minced
1 T parsley
1 t basil
1½ t salt

2 1 lb cans of Italian tomatoes
2 6oz. cans tomato paste

If using sausage, slice it lengthwise. In any event brown the meat slowly, drain fat. Add other ingredients and simmer uncovered until thick, stirring once or twice for at least an hour — two to two and a half are better.

I sometimes add sliced mushrooms if I have them.

If you add the garlic after the meat is browned, it won't smell up the kitchen as it cooks.

Scargo Lasagne

1 recipe basic spaghetti sauce

10 oz. lasagne noodles - cook-drain and
  rinse in cold water-lay on paper
  towels to dry

3 c ricotta
2 beaten eggs
2 t salt
½ t pepper
2 T parsley, chopped
½ c parmesan cheese

Mix all these
ingredients
together

½ lb. mozzarella cheese
  sliced

Beginning with a small amount of sauce
in a greased casserole or shallow
pan, layer noodles, cheese mixture,
mozzarella, sauce, ending with a
few noodles and sauce on top.
This can be done a day ahead.

Bake at 375° for 30 minutes if
hot - about an hour if cold. Let
stand 15 minutes before cutting
in squares.

This freezes well. Serves at least 8.

Company Casserole

A distant cousin of lasagne, I guess. It started with a recipe from the Provincetown paper and was changed a bit along the way.

1 recipe basic spaghetti sauce — with 1 8oz. can mushrooms and 1/2 c red wine added. Cook over low heat until thick.

1 8oz. package green noodles, cooked and drained.

2 3oz. packages cream cheese
1/3 c milk
2 t lemon juice
1/4 t garlic salt
1 t worcestershire
} Mix until smooth and add noodles.

1/4 c parmesan

Alternate layers of noodle mixture and meat mixture in a 2 1/2 quart casserole. Sprinkle top with the parmesan cheese and dot with butter. Bake at 350° 40 minutes to an hour until bubbly and browned. Serves 6-8.

Smothered Hamburger and Onions

The ways with hamburger are legion. This is one of my husband's favorites and does wonders for the budget — ½ lb. feeds two well.

½ lb. ground chuck
¼ c water or wine
½ t salt
pinch pepper

¼ c fine dry bread crumbs
2 medium onions sliced
½ can beef gravy

Mix the first five ingredients and shape into two large oval patties about ½ inch thick. Sprinkle a frying pan that has a lid (electric skillet is great) with ½ t salt (add no fat) and pan broil the patties just until brown. When you turn them add the onions and brown lightly. Add the gravy (a T of the wine used in the patties is a nice touch). Cover and simmer about 35 minutes.

Serves 2.

This is good with mashed potatoes.

Pot Roasted Meat Loaf

1 lb. ground beef
⅔ c evaporated milk
⅓ c fine dry bread crumbs
1 t salt

¼ t pepper
¼ c catsup or chili sauce (I prefer the latter)
2 t worcestershire

3 medium potatoes and
3 medium onions each peeled and sliced ¼ inch thick

3 medium carrots peeled and quartered

2 t parsley flakes

1 t salt
⅛ t pepper

In a large bowl, mix the beef, milk, bread crumbs, catsup, salt and pepper, and worcestershire. Shape into a loaf in the center of a 13 x 9 x 2 pan. Put the sliced vegetables in layers around the meat, and sprinkle each layer with a mixture of the parsley flakes, salt and pepper. Cover with foil.

Bake at 375° for 1 hour, or until

the vegetables are tender. Uncover
and bake 10 minutes more to
brown meat.   Serves 4.

Flu Stew

This evolved from necessity — a
well husband and sick me.

1 lb. stew meat — preferably beef
1 can cream of mushroom soup
½ soup can red wine

2 T instant onion — or ½ package
            dry onion soup mix

Salt and pepper — go lightly on the
      salt — the soup takes care of it

¼ t basil — if you are feeling devilish

Put it all in a casserole — raw
meat and all, cover, put the
casserole in a 275° to 300° oven.
Go away and leave it to fend
for itself for 3-4 hours — 5 if
the casserole has a very tight
lid (aluminum foil under the
regular lid, please).

Serve it over rice.   Serves 2-3.

Roast Lamb

My favorite roasting method: Preheat oven to 450°. Put meat on rack in an uncovered pan. Put in oven. Immediately reduce heat to 350°. Roast 30 minutes a pound.

I Stick the top of the meat with whole cloves. Sprinkle with a mixture of 3T brown sugar and 1 T marjoram— then roast.

II Sliver a clove of garlic. Punch tiny holes in meat and insert garlic. Rub meat well with equal parts lemon juice and oil mixed. Let stand 1 hour—then roast.

Braised Lamb Chops with Vegetables

2 ½ lb. shoulder lamb (or veal) chops
2 medium potatoes pared and quartered
2 medium carrots cut in 1 inch pieces
1 stalk celery cut in 1 inch pieces
½ t salt
¼ t marjoram (or basil)
½ c water

Brown chops in a heavy skillet with a lid in their own fat. Sprinkling the pan with salt

40

first keeps them from sticking. Drain off all fat. Put the vegetables around and over the chops. Sprinkle with salt and herb. Add water, cover. Cook over low heat for 45 minutes until chops and vegetables are tender.   Serves 2.

Lamb Chops Creole

2 large or 4 small shoulder lamb chops
1 t oil   1/8 t pepper
1 small onion diced   3/4 t salt
1/4 c diced green pepper   1/8 t chili powder
1 1/4 c canned tomatoes   (if you have it)
   (well drained)

Brown the chops in a heavy skillet sprinkled with salt — then remove to a casserole.

Wipe out the skillet — add oil — heat and add green pepper and onion. Brown lightly and add tomatoes and seasonings. Stir well and simmer a few minutes. Pour over chops and bake tightly covered in a 350° oven for 1 hour.   Serves 2.

Shepherd's Pie

1 lb. ground lamb* or leftover roast lamb
1 onion diced
1 clove garlic minced
2 T flour
1¼ c water or gravy
¼ c cold coffee
2 carrots sliced
2 stalks celery sliced
½ c peas, corn or mixed vegetables
¼ t basil
1 T parsley minced
2 c mashed potatoes

*Ground lamb is sold as lamb patties and is fairly inexpensive.

Brown meat in a heavy skillet, spooning off all but 1 T fat as it accumulates. While the meat is browning, simmer the carrots and celery until almost tender. (I use the water from this to make the gravy.)

When meat is almost done add onion and garlic and brown. Sprinkle this mixture with flour and brown the flour. Add water or gravy and coffee and stir until thickened.

Add vegetables to the meat mixture and sprinkle with parsley and basil. Put in a casserole and top with mashed potatoes. Dot with butter, sprinkle with paprika and bake at 375° 35-40 minutes.   Serves 4.

Pan Broiled Lamb Chops

Using shoulder lamb chops (does your market call them fore-quarter chops?) - trim excess fat - Sprinkle well with meat tenderizer - following label directions. Sprinkle a pre-heated skillet well with salt (do not add any fat or oil). Cook chops 8 minutes on first side. Stand up on edge to brown fat and then turn and cook 5-7 minutes on the second side. Spoon off fat as it accumulates. Quick, easy and good!

⁂

Oven Barbecued Lamb Roast

1 3lb. shank half of lamb leg	
1 t ginger	2 T chili sauce
1 t dry mustard	1 T worcestershire
1/2 t salt	1 T vinegar
1/4 t pepper	2 T oil
1 onion sliced	1 c boiling water

Mix ginger, mustard, salt and pepper and rub into meat. Put roast on a rack in a shallow pan and lay onion slices on the meat. Mix the last five ingredients, and roast the meat at 300° for 30 minutes a pound basting often with this sauce.

Horizon Hill Baked Ham

One of my vacation recipes — this one named for a lovely old farm near Mt. Monadnock where it was initiated.

½ ham *
¾ c apple cider
¾ c maple syrup
   whole cloves

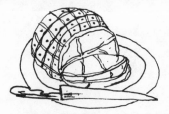

Remove heavy skin with a sharp knife. Score the ham in diamond shapes and stick with cloves immediately. Bake at 300° for ½ hour a pound. Baste every 20 minutes (or when you think of it) with cider - syrup mixture.

*I usually buy a shank-half (easier to carve). For the two of us, I ask the butcher to cut off a one inch slice for another meal.

The ham is good with scalloped or au gratin potatoes and a great company dish as it is good hot, warm or cold. Wonderful to have in the refrigerator for sandwiches, casseroles or just "as is", it is also known as a "set-piece" in summer — the more you can "set" the "peacefuller" you get.

Ham and Broccoli

My private definition of eternity is "a ham and two people" – this is a favorite way of using some of the leftovers.

2 packages frozen broccoli spears (or fresh if you would rather) cooked lightly and well drained
1 10 oz. can cream of mushroom soup
¼ c milk
2 T sherry
Slices of ham
¼ C grated sharp cheese
crumbs (packaged stuffing mix, bread crumbs or whatever)

Lay the broccoli in a shallow baking dish, cover with slices of ham. Mix soup, milk and sherry and pour over all. Top with crumbs and the grated cheese. Bake at 350° for 25 minutes or until bubbly and lightly browned.   Serves 4.

Substitute asparagus, whole green beans or lima beans for broccoli if you like (or if the ham lasts that long).

Dry Marinated Roast Pork

A new addition to my repertoire (I never stop trying).

½ pork loin (5-6 ribs) trimmed of heavy fat

oil

3 t salt

¼ t pepper

¾ t sage and thyme mixed

1 bay leaf crumbled

1 t ground allspice

1 clove garlic mashed

1 onion sliced

1 carrot sliced

Bouquet garni (parsley, thyme and a bay leaf)

½ c dry vermouth

Mix salt, pepper, herbs, spices and garlic and rub into meat. Cover, but plan to turn the meat several times. I let it sit at room temperature for several hours, refrigerate if overnight. Before cooking scrape the marinade off the meat and dry well with paper towels.

Heat oil to almost smoking and brown meat well on all sides (this takes at least 10 minutes). Put meat fat side up in a casserole just large enough to hold it. Lightly brown the onion and carrot in fat remaining in the pan and add to meat with the bouquet garni. Cover and roast for 40 minutes per pound at 325°, basting occasionally with the accumulating liquid.

When done, remove meat to a warm platter, skim liquid and mash the vegetables into it. Add the wine and rapidly boil down to 1 cup. Strain into gravy boat.

The faint spiciness of the meat makes it lovely for a cold meat as well.

Serves 4.

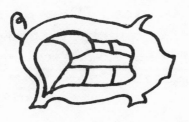

Better cross an angry man than a hungry man.

Danish proverb

Chinese Pork and Broccoli

1½-2 c leftover roast pork diced
  in fairly large cubes
oil
1 t salt   1½ T cornstarch
⅛ t pepper   ¼ c water
1½ c chicken broth   1½ t soy sauce*
1 onion sliced thin
1 c celery sliced thin
1 package frozen broccoli stalks
  cut in 1 inch pieces

Heat oil and lightly brown pork cubes.
Add salt, pepper, broth and onion.
Cover and cook 10 minutes. Add
celery and broccoli. Cover and cook
5 minutes. Blend cornstarch, water
and soy sauce, add to meat
mixture and cook until thickened.

Serve with rice. The advent of
unexpected guests has on occasion
prompted the addition of Chinese
fried noodles, the canned
variety.   Serves 4.

*The difference in soy sauce
is amazing and the imported
Japanese sauce makes all
the difference.

48

Oven Barbecued Pork Chops

4 pork chops — I use "end cut" and
   trim excess fat — they are a lot
   less expensive

½ c catsup or
   chili sauce
1 t salt
1 t celery seed
½ t nutmeg
⅓ c vinegar
1 c water
   1 bay leaf

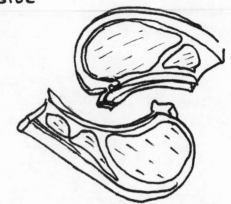

Brown the chops in a heavy skillet
sprinkled with salt. Remove to
a casserole. Wipe out skillet.
Mix all of the other ingredients
and pour into skillet. Simmer a
minute or two, stirring to deglaze
pan. Pour sauce over the chops.
Cover tightly and bake at 325°
for 1½ hours.   Serves 2 well.

We like baked potatoes with
this.

If you have sauce left over it
is very good for barbecuing
hot dogs.

Baked Pork Chops with Sour Cream

A fairly new addition to our table, this is also good with veal chops.

2 pork chops (I sometimes buy pork steak or fillets if I can - they are leaner)

Insert a whole clove in each. Brown lightly in a salted pan. Place in a baking dish and pour this mixture over the meat:

1 T vinegar
1½ t sugar
¼ c sour cream
(or plain yogurt)

¼ c water or stock
(mixed with a little
wine if you like)
½ bay leaf

Bake in a preheated 350° oven for 1 hour.

Bay

This is good with baked potatoes or rice (the gravy deserves them) and a green vegetable - or - for a change - baked acorn squash (see page 93) and a green salad.

Veal Bolognese

4 small veal steaks or cutlets (I now use chopped veal patties, unbreaded,)

Seasoned flour
2 T olive oil divided
1 T butter
1 onion chopped
a few mushrooms
   sliced
1 clove garlic minced

1 8oz can tomato
   sauce
1/4 t basil
1/4 c grated Romano
   or Parmesan cheese
2 slices swiss or
   provolone cheese

Sprinkle the meat with seasoned flour and brown in 1T hot oil. While the meat browns, heat the butter and remaining oil and in it lightly brown the onion, garlic, and mushrooms. Add the tomato sauce and basil and simmer 10 minutes.

Put a tablespoon or two of sauce in a shallow baking dish and spread it around. Arrange meat on this – it may overlap. Pour in sauce and sprinkle with grated cheese and lay strips of swiss down the center. Heat in 400° oven till bubbly and browned, about 15 to 20 minutes.   Serves 2.

Neapolitan Veal and Peppers

2/3 lb. veal cutlet sliced thin and cut
   in 3 inch pieces
2 large green peppers
1/3 c olive oil
1 clove garlic minced
1/2 t salt
1/4 t pepper
1 lb. can whole peeled tomatoes
   well drained
1/8 t oregano
1/2 t chopped pimento
4-5 green olives, pitted and cut up (I
   use stuffed olives-chop pimento
   and slice olives lengthwise

Cut peppers in halves, remove seeds
and membranes and slice coarsely.
Heat oil in a heavy skillet and
brown veal well. Add peppers and
garlic and sauté over low heat
for 5 minutes. Add crushed
tomato pulp, salt and pepper
and cook together for 15 minutes.
Add olives, pimento and oregano
and simmer 2 more minutes.
                    Serves 2.

This is good alone but goes
especially well with green
noodles.

52

Summer Corned Beef Loaf

I first made this for a picnic at a friend's farm in the Connecticut hills. Each time I serve it now I think of that happy luncheon on the terrace under the grape arbor.

1 envelope plain gelatin
1 can consommé
1 t catsup
1 T sherry
¼ c water
½ t horseradish
¼ t salt
fresh ground pepper
¾ c mayonnaise

3 hard-boiled eggs chopped
1 c celery chopped
½ c sliced almonds
2 T green pepper finely chopped
⅓ c pitted ripe olives chopped
1 12 oz can corned beef finely chopped

In a saucepan sprinkle gelatin over ½ c of the consommé to soften. Put over low heat and stir constantly until the gelatin is dissolved. Remove from heat and add the rest of the consommé, the catsup, sherry, water, horseradish, salt and pepper. Stir well. Chill, stirring frequently until it is completely cold but has not yet begun to thicken.

Blend in the mayonnaise with a rotary beater. Fold in the remaining ingredients. Rinse an 8½ x 4½ x 2½ loaf pan in cold water, pour in the mixture and chill overnight.

Unmold on salad greens and garnish with green pepper slices and sliced tomatoes.   Serves 6-8.

I always serve Remoulade Sauce (see page 14) with this.

"With money anyone can offer succulent dishes and famous wines, but courtesy and kindness cannot be bought."

Lucien Tendret

Chicken

"Poultry is for the cook
what canvas is
for the painter."

Morrison Wood

Approximate Timetable for Roasting

			unstuffed (hours)	stuffed (hours)
Broiler-Fryer whole	1½ - 2 lbs.	400°	¾ - 1	1 - 1½
	2 - 2½ lbs.	400°	1 - 1½	1½ - 1¾
	2½ - 3 lbs.	400°	1½ - 2	2 - 2½
	3 - 4 lbs.	400°	2 - 2½	2½ - 3
Roaster	3½ - 6 lbs.	375°	3 - 3½	3½ - 4
Cornish Hen	1 - 2 lbs.	400°	1	1 - 1¼
Capon	6 - 8 lbs.	350°	3 - 3½	3½ - 4½

Use a shallow open pan. Rub the bird with oil or unsalted fat. Baste if you like - I usually do - at least for the last half hour. Plan to have the bird out of the oven 15 - 20 minutes before you want to eat so the juices can set.

I often just sprinkle the inside of the bird with salt and pepper (maybe a pinch of an herb), put in an onion cut in quarters, a stalk of celery, a carrot and a sprig of parsley and roast as usual.

It is just as easy to cook two broiler-fryers at once — then you have another "set-piece"!

My Own Broiled Chicken

Split a broiler in half by running a knife (or kitchen shears) down one side of backbone. Put chicken on a flat surface — give it a good whack to snap bones — snap out breast bone. Remove backbone (use in stock pot). Finish cutting in halves.

If you have the time, marinate the chicken in oil and vinegar salad dressing for a while, otherwise just drizzle liberally with dressing and broil skin side down. Salt, then turn and broil skin side up. I find about 6 inches away from my broiler is fine — 20 minutes on the first side. The second side — "so it shouldn't burn" — maybe 10-15 minutes.

This is especially good if you force butter between the skin and the meat before cooking.

If chickens are small you might want to try putting an ice cube on the ribs when you do the first side. When it has melted and the chicken browned — turn it. Crazy but it works!

Stewed Chicken

This is delicious as is — even better the second day, so do make it a day ahead, but, please, skin it while it is hot! I find good cooked chicken the basis for so many things.

4 lb. stewing chicken cut up
1 C white wine
water
1 medium onion quartered
3 stalks celery
3 carrots quartered
1 sprig parsley
1 bay leaf
6 peppercorns
1/8 t marjoram
2 t salt

Put the chicken and all other ingredients but the water in a large pan with a tight cover. Add enough water to just come to the top of the meat. Cover and simmer gently for 2 hours, or until tender. Thicken broth if you like — I rarely bother. Unless you plan to use it immediately, skin and cool in broth.

During the twelve years I worked, I often made this on Saturday mornings. It cooked while I did other things.

We particularly like it served in a deep dish with the vegetables and some very fine noodles called "Fideos" and lots of broth. Soupy but good. I cook the "Fideos" in some of the broth.

Herb Baked Chicken

My herb garden is a great source of both contentment and flavor. This is a lovely use of some of its harvest.

1 whole broiler 2½ - 3 lbs.	⅓ c melted butter or margarine
1 t garlic salt	⅓ c dry white wine
2 t crushed rosemary, divided	½ t crushed basil ½ t salt and pepper

Wash and dry the chicken. Sprinkle neck and body cavities with garlic salt and 1 t rosemary. Combine the butter, wine, other 1 t rosemary, basil, salt and pepper. Truss the chicken and put in shallow roasting pan. Brush with the wine-butter sauce. Bake at 400° for 1½ - 2 hours brushing several times with the sauce. Remove trussing and carve.   Serves 4.

Chicken Tetrazzini

A favorite use of the stewed chicken,
I have made this for as many as forty
people, and can vouch for the fact that
if your pans are large enough it octuples
beautifully. (I had help with the math!)
For three try it this way.

¼ lb green noodles cooked   1 T sherry
1 c mushrooms sliced   1-2 c cooked
2 T butter   chicken cubed
2 c Velouté Sauce*   ⅓ c grated
⅛ t nutmeg   parmesan

Sauté mushrooms in butter. Season
the sauce with nutmeg and sherry.
Put the noodles in a shallow dish. Add
half the sauce. Put in chicken and
mushrooms. Pour in rest of sauce.
Sprinkle with cheese. Bake at 400°
35-40 minutes.

* Velouté Sauce

2⅓ T butter   ⅓ t salt
4 T flour   few grains pepper
1⅓ c chicken broth   ½ c evaporated milk

Melt butter, add flour, blend well, add
broth stirring constantly. Bring to boil
and boil 2 minutes. Add evaporated milk.

Baked Broilers with Stuffing

We arrived home one night to find a good friend in the living room. "My wife just had a boy and I was hungry and lonely!" My husband made a brimming glass, while I reached hurriedly for:

2 broilers split
½ package stuffing mix
⅓ c water and sherry
   to make ½ c
1 small onion diced

1 stalk celery sliced
⅓ c melted butter
⅓ c sherry
Salt and pepper
½ t poultry seasoning

Mix stuffing according to directions using the ½ c of water and sherry, and adding onion and celery. In a 13 x 9 x 2 baking dish, spoon stuffing into four mounds. Lay one-half broiler over each mound. Mix melted butter and sherry and pour over chicken halves. Sprinkle with salt, pepper and poultry seasoning. Cover with foil and put in a 375° oven for 40 minutes. Uncover. Baste with pan juices and bake 20 minutes longer until crisp and brown.

We had a lovely evening. If you are lazy like me, you put a few potatoes in to bake with the chicken and toss a salad. Great! Serves 4.

Chicken alla Cacciatora

What I would like to know is, how did those hunters always happen to have a tomato or two in their game bags?

1 broiler cut up
Seasoned flour
2 T olive oil
1 medium onion chopped
1 stalk celery minced
1 whole clove garlic*
a few sliced mushrooms
1 pimento diced
1/4 t sugar
a pinch of cinnamon
    or allspice
2 T sherry or 1/4 c red wine
1/2 c tomato juice or sauce,
    or 2 tomatoes cut up

Sprinkle chicken with seasoned flour. Brown lightly in oil. Remove chicken from the pan, and add onion, celery, garlic, mushrooms and pimento. Stir and cook until onion is yellow. Add sugar, spice and chicken. Add wine. Cook and stir for 5 minutes. * Remove garlic. Add tomatoes. Cover and cook slowly until chicken is tender (40 to 60 minutes). If necessary, add more liquid from time to time, using chicken broth, wine or tomato juice. Season to taste.   Serves 4.

Mrs. Greene's Chicken and Rice

1 broiler-fryer cut up	1 t poultry seasoning
1 C uncooked rice	1/2 c mayonnaise or
1 4 oz. can mushrooms	salad dressing
2 c + chicken broth	1/2 t salt

Butter a large casserole. Drain the mushrooms, reserving liquid. Put rice and mushrooms in casserole and mix. Put mushroom liquid in cup and add chicken broth to make 2½c. Pour over rice. Mix salt, poultry seasoning and mayonnaise and spread on chicken, coating well. Lay chicken on rice in casserole (it looks messy) Bake for 1 hour - or more- at 375°.   Serves 4.

For some reason the chicken browns beautifully, the rice grains separate and it tastes marvelous.

Breast of Chicken In White Wine

12 whole chicken breasts split, boned and skinned
½ lb. butter or margarine
2 C onion finely chopped
½ lb. small mushrooms
2 c garlic crushed
½ c flour
½ t each thyme leaves, salt and pepper
2 13¾ oz. cans chicken broth

4 chicken bouillon cubes
2 c sauterne

In a 5 quart dutch oven melt some of the butter and brown breasts a few at a time, adding butter as needed. Remove all breasts from pan. Add onion, mushrooms and garlic, sauté stirring 5 minutes. Remove from heat. Combine flour, thyme, salt and pepper. Stir into onion mixture. Gradually stir in broth and crumble in bouillon cubes. Bring to a boil, stirring constantly, reduce heat and add wine. Preheat oven to 400°. Add breasts to wine mixture; bake, 50 minutes. Uncover, stir and continue baking for 15 minutes.

*To freeze: bake 30 minutes only. Foil line casseroles, fold foil over chicken

and freeze until solid. Remove from
casserole. Freezer wrap.

To serve: unwrap, place in the same
casserole, thaw completely. Bake in a
400° oven 40 minutes (or 375° 1 hour)
covered; stir, bake 15 minutes longer
uncovered.   Garnish with parsley.
Serves 16-18

Italian (almost) Baked Chicken

This is a nice change from fried
chicken. It is good hot, or it makes
a lovely addition to a picnic cold.

2 broilers cut up
1½ t salt
1 can condensed tomato soup
⅓ c water

1½ c cornflake
crumbs
½ c parmesan
2 t oregano

Sprinkle chicken with salt. Mix soup
and water in one pie pan, mix crumbs,
cheese and oregano in another. Dip
chicken pieces first in soup, then
roll in crumb mixture to coat well.
Bake on foil-lined baking sheets —
skin side up at 350° for 40 minutes.
Do not turn chicken over but turn
pans around in oven and bake
40 minutes longer.   Serves 6.

Chicken à la Brandon

My mother does this just with chicken breasts, I use broiler-fryers cut up.

2 broiler-fryers cut up
3 T oil or butter
2 onions chopped
½ lb mushrooms sliced
1 T flour
1 10 oz can cream of
  mushroom soup

¼ c milk
¼ c white wine or
  sherry
½ t each thyme, sage,
  salt and pepper
1 t parsley
¼ c sliced almonds

Brown the chicken in oil or butter. Be sure the chicken is dry – do not crowd the pan, and stand back – it spatters. As the chicken is browned, remove to a casserole. Add more oil to the pan if there is not 2T remaining and sauté the onions and the mushrooms until lightly browned. Sprinkle in the flour and stir for a minute or two to cook flour. Add soup and milk, stirring until smooth. Add wine, herbs, salt and pepper. Pour this sauce over the chicken and sprinkle with almonds.

At this point it can go in the refrigerator overnight — or right into a preheated 350° oven for 45 minutes to an hour.

If it has been refrigerated, put in a cold oven. Set oven at 350° and bake 1½ hours.
Serves 8.

Fish

"They say fish
    should swim thrice...

first it should swim
    in the sea,

then it should swim
    in butter,

    and at last, sirrah,
it should swim in claret."

          J. Swift

Baked Fish Chowder

2 lbs. haddock fillets
4 potatoes sliced
½ c sliced celery tops
1 bay leaf
2½ t salt
3 whole cloves
3 onions sliced
    chopped parsley

4 T butter
¼ t dill seed
¼ t white pepper
½ c dry white wine
2 c boiling water
2 c milk or undiluted
    evaporated milk

Put all ingredients except the milk and parsley in a 3 quart casserole. Cover and bake in a 375° oven for 1 hour. Heat milk to scalding. Add to the chowder. Garnish with parsley.

I have been known to dice salt pork in ¼ inch cubes – try them out well – discard drippings and use the cubes for garnish. If you do this use only a tablespoon or two of butter.

Serves 6.

Split and toasted common crackers, a good sharp cheese, and green salad make this a hearty and different meal.

Bluefish with Barbecue Sauce

I find fish not only good - we love it - but a real help to the budget.*

2 lbs. bluefish or haddock fillets

Make a sauce of:

1 1/2 T olive oil	2 1/2 T catsup
1 small clove garlic crushed	1 T orange juice
1 T onion chopped	1/4 t pepper
1 1/2 t soy sauce	1/4 t oregano

Put fish skin side down on broiler rack. Pour sauce over fish. Broil 2 inches from heat for 4-6 minutes without turning, until fish loses its transparent look and separates into large flakes when tested. Don't over cook it!

Serves 4.

I have found that rinsing fresh or frozen fish in salted water and then patting dry with paper towels before proceeding with any recipe really freshens the fish.

*For a simpler meal drizzle equal parts oil and lemon juice over split fish and broil as above.

69

Sea Food Casserole

A favorite buffet dish for a party — a bit expensive, but awfully good.

½ c butter
½ c flour
4 c milk
¾ lb. sharp cheese grated and divided
2 t salt
¼ t each paprika and basil
1 8-oz. box noodles cooked

4 ozs. pimentos
½ lb. mushrooms sliced
1 6½ oz. can lobster
1 6½ oz. can crab
½ lb. shrimp cooked and cleaned
1 c dry stuffing mix crumbled

Make a cream sauce using the butter, flour and milk. Season it with salt, basil and paprika and melt in two-thirds of the cheese. Dice the pimentos and sauté with the mushrooms. Drain the crab and lobster and pick over both for bits of shell or tendons. Mix all together in a large buttered casserole. (This should have a lovely pink color, if not, add a bit more paprika). Sprinkle top with stuffing mix and the remaining cheese, dot with butter. Bake at 350° for 1 hour.   Serves 6-8.

I use a green salad garnished with croutons and a good hot bread to complete the meal.

Flounder Fillets Au Fromage

¾ lb. flounder fillets
½ t salt
dash pepper
1 T chopped onion
2 T melted butter

1 c soft bread cubes
¼ c sharp cheese grated
3 T milk
1 T sherry

Sprinkle fillets with salt and pepper. Put in a single layer in a well-greased baking dish. Cook onion in butter until tender. Add the bread cubes and cheese. Mix well and spread over fish. Pour milk and wine around fish. Bake at 350° for 20 minutes. Serves 2.

Flounder Fillets En Casserole

¾ lb. flounder fillets
½ c soft bread crumbs
1½ t vinegar
1½ t worcestershire
1½ t lemon juice

½ t salt
¼ t pepper
¼ c melted butter
   or margarine
½ t mustard

Cover bottom of a greased baking dish with crumbs and lay fish on them. Make a sauce of the other ingredients, beating them into the melted butter. Pour over the fish. Bake at 300° for 20 minutes, basting with the sauce occasionally.   Serves 2.

South Wellfleet Striped Bass

There is no thrill like your first strike when surf fishing. My husband was lucky, and we had striper for dinner.

2 lb. bass fillets
1/4 lb. butter or margarine divided
1/2 t salt

1/4 t fresh ground pepper
1/3 c dry white wine
1/8 t garlic salt

Butter a baking dish quite heavily and lay the fish on the butter. Sprinkle with salt and pepper, dot with half the remaining butter. Pour on the wine and bake at 350° for 15 minutes. Melt the remaining butter and add garlic salt. Pour over the fish and bake another 5 minutes, basting once or twice with the juices in the pan. Serves 4.

Shrimp In Wine Sauce

A beautiful chafing dish specialty:

3/4 lb. shrimp, shelled and cleaned, but raw
1 T flour
1/2 t salt
1/4 t fresh ground pepper
1 T butter

a scant 1/2 c dry white wine
1 T hot water
1 t tomato paste
1 minced scallion
minced parsley

Toss shrimp in flour seasoned with salt and pepper. Melt butter and sauté shrimp about 2 minutes on each side. Combine wine, water, tomato paste and scallion and mix into shrimp. Cook over low heat 5 minutes. Sprinkle with parsley.

We like this with rice.   Serves 2.

Baked Stuffed Clams

2 7½ oz. cans minced clams
4 T butter divided
3 T flour
½ c clam juice
½ c milk
1 T grated onion
¼ t each basil, sage and thyme

½ t salt
¼ t pepper
1 T minced parsley
1 t lemon juice or more
dash tabasco
1 c or more dry stuffing mix divided
¼ c grated sharp cheese

Drain the clams reserving their juice, and chop finer. Make a sauce with 3T butter, flour, clam juice and milk. Season highly with herbs, salt, pepper, lemon juice and tabasco. Add the clams and enough of the stuffing mix to make a thick mixture. Butter baking shells and fill. Sprinkle with stuffing mix and cheese. Dot with butter. Bake at 425° for 15 minutes until bubbly and browned. Serves 8 as an appetizer— 4 for a main course.

73

Scalloped Clams Elizabeth

2 7½ oz. cans
  minced clams
4 T margarine or
  butter divided
1 stalk celery
  minced
1 onion minced
¼ c parsley
½ box soda
  crackers

½ c light cream
  or milk
½ c clam juice
½ t lemon juice
fresh ground
  pepper

Drain the clams, reserving juice.
Melt 1 T of the butter and sauté
the onion, celery and parsley until
lightly browned. Melt the remaining
butter and crumble the crackers
into it. Line a greased baking
dish with some of the crumbs,
then a layer of clams, sautéed
vegetables, and crumbs, ending
with a layer of crumbs. Sprinkle
each layer of clams with a grind
of pepper. Mix cream, clam juice
and lemon juice and pour over.
Dot with butter. Bake at 350°
for 25-30 minutes until it is
browned on top.

This serves 6-8 as a first
course, 3-4 as a main dish.

Shrimp Louisiane

One of my first party recipes; I've made it many times and for as many as twelve.

1 lb. shrimp cooked and shelled	1 1-lb. can tomatoes
1 T butter	few grains cayenne or dash hot pepper sauce
1 T flour	Salt (try ½ t and taste after adding shrimp)
1 onion chopped	
1 green pepper in thin slivers	¼ t basil
	1 bay leaf
¼ c parsley minced	2 t worcestershire

Melt butter, add flour and brown lightly. In this roux, cook onion, green pepper and parsley until lightly brown. Add tomatoes, stirring constantly until tomato juices are thickened and smooth. Add seasonings and herbs. Simmer ½ hour, stirring occasionally, until flavors are blended. Just before serving add shrimp and heat a minute or two. Stir in the worcestershire. Serve over rice to 4.

All you need with this is a salad, and once more, I love it for entertaining — as the shrimp are not added until the last moment there is no danger of their becoming tough.

75

Swordfish Mayonnaise

I have served this to people who don't really like fish and received raves — another oven recipe.

2 lbs. swordfish or halibut steak	½-¾ c mayonnaise
1 t salt	1½ t instant onion
¼ t fresh ground pepper	¾ c corn flake crumbs

Season fish with salt and pepper. Spread generously with mayonnaise and lay in a greased baking dish just large enough to hold it. Sprinkle with the instant onion, then with the crumbs. Bake at 400° 30 minutes.   Serves 4.

We like bread and butter pickles with this.

"To invite someone is to take charge of his happiness during the time he spends under your roof."
                    Brillat-Savarin

Cheese
And Other
Good Things

"Many's the long night I've
dreamed of cheese —
toasted mostly."

R.L. Stevenson

Cheese Soufflé Bain Marie

Don't panic at the word "soufflé". For some unknown reason this lovely stays up once it gets there, and even reheats the same double boiler way.

2 T butter or margarine
2 T flour
½ t dry mustard
½ t salt
1 c milk
1 c grated swiss
   or cheddar cheese
4 eggs, separated

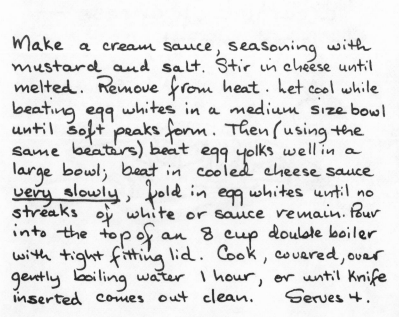

Make a cream sauce, seasoning with mustard and salt. Stir in cheese until melted. Remove from heat. Let cool while beating egg whites in a medium size bowl until soft peaks form. Then (using the same beaters) beat egg yolks well in a large bowl; beat in cooled cheese sauce <u>very slowly</u>, fold in egg whites until no streaks of white or sauce remain. Pour into the top of an 8 cup double boiler with tight fitting lid. Cook, covered, over gently boiling water 1 hour, or until knife inserted comes out clean.   Serves 4.

Cheese Fondue Casserole

Upon occasion my husband has been heard to ask for "cheese pud" for dinner. This is what he had in mind. You may substitute white wine or beer for part of the milk if you like.

6 slices bread, buttered and cubed	few grains cayenne
2½ c grated sharp cheese	⅛ t each cloves, thyme and nutmeg
3 eggs	¼ t worcestershire
2½ c milk	¼ t prepared mustard
1 t salt	

Layer the bread and cheese in a buttered casserole having cheese for the top layer. Beat the eggs until light, add the remaining ingredients and blend thoroughly. Pour over the bread and cheese, let stand for at least ½ hour, then bake in a 300° - 325° oven 1 hour or until a knife inserted in the middle comes out clean.

Serves 4.

Steamed spinach (or beet greens) goes nicely with this, and, for a salad, thick slices of tomato sprinkled with oregano, salt and pepper and drizzled with an oil and vinegar dressing.

Horizon Hill Macaroni and Cheese

This is the companion piece to the baked ham also named for Horizon Hill.

½ lb. butter or margarine
1 onion minced
½ c flour
2 t salt
¼ t fresh ground pepper
½ t each sage and basil
1 t parsley minced
1 t dry mustard

1 T worcestershire
4 c milk
1 12 oz. bottle beer (or equivalent extra milk)
¾ lb. sharp cheddar grated and divided
1 lb. elbow macaroni cooked
1 c dry stuffing mix

Melt the butter in a heavy pan and in it brown the onion. Add flour, salt, pepper, herbs, mustard and worcestershire. Blend well until smooth. Simmer a minute or two, stirring constantly. Remove from heat and slowly add the milk and beer. (I find that a wire whip smoothes sauces much more rapidly than a spoon.) Cook over medium heat, stirring constantly until thickened. Turn heat low and add two-thirds of the cheese. Stir constantly until melted. Be careful, it scorches easily. Pour sauce over macaroni in a large greased casserole. Mix well (it looks quite soupy). Top with stuffing

mix and remaining cheese. Dot with
butter and sprinkle with paprika.

Bake until bubbly and browned:
  in a 300° oven 1½ - 2 hours,
  in a 325° oven 1 - 1½ hours, or
  in a 350° oven 1 hour.
The "vat size" takes the longer time.

Serves 12.

You can cut the recipe in half for
six or double it (as I do) for about
twenty-five.

Olive and Egg Loaf

12 <u>hot</u> hard-boiled eggs	2 T minced onion
½ c butter softened	1 t salt
⅓ c celery diced	¼ t fresh ground
¼ c pimento-stuffed	pepper
olives chopped	¼ t basil

Peel the eggs under running cold water. Put
in a large bowl and mash with a potato
masher until they are coarsely chopped.
Stir in the rest of the ingredients.

Line a 5 cup loaf pan with buttered wax
paper and press in egg mixture. Chill 6
hours or overnight. Unmold on salad
greens and garnish with green pepper
rings and sliced tomatoes.   Serves 8.

Noodles Romanov

A blender recipe that goes together while the noodles cook.

¼ lb. egg noodles cooked and tossed with
   1½ T butter
1 slice bread
½ c American or
   cheddar cheese
½ c sour cream
1 c cottage cheese

1 small onion
   diced
1 clove garlic cut
1 t salt
dash tabasco

In blender container put bread and cheese. Blend 30 seconds. Remove to a small bowl. Place remaining ingredients in container. Blend until smooth. Pour this over the noodles and stir lightly to combine. Pour into a buttered casserole. Drift crumb mixture over top. Bake at 350° for 30 minutes.

Serves 6.

This takes kindly to mixing with some browned hamburger, leftover chicken, diced ham, tuna, shrimp, vienna sausages — or what you will. It then becomes a main dish for three or four — but don't then call it "Romanov," my Russian friends would die.

82

Conchiglie (Shells) Florentine

24 giant macaroni shells
    cooked, drained and
    rinsed in cool water
3 c tomato sauce (see
    Veal Bolognese, page 51
    or use a meatless
    spaghetti sauce)
½ c celery chopped
2 T chopped onion
1 T oil
1 10 oz. package frozen
    chopped spinach, cooked
    and very well drained

2 C cottage cheese
1 beaten egg
½ c grated parmesan
    cheese divided
¼ c fine dry bread
    crumbs
¼ t oregano
¼ t basil
⅛ t nutmeg
½ t salt
1 slice swiss or
    muenster cheese
    shredded

Cook onion and celery in oil until tender.
Turn into a large bowl. Add spinach, cottage
cheese, egg, ¼ c parmesan, crumbs, nutmeg,
herbs and salt. Combine well. Fill shells and
put in a shallow oiled casserole in which you
have spread a few tablespoons of tomato
sauce. Pour the rest of the sauce around
and over the filled shells. Sprinkle with the
remaining ¼ c parmesan. Cover with foil.
Bake at 375° 30 minutes. Remove foil,
put shredded swiss cheese on top of shells
and bake uncovered 15 minutes longer.
                  Serves 4.
These freeze beautifully.

Eggplant Romano

1 eggplant
Salt
3T (or more) oil
1 clove garlic minced
1½ c tomato sauce

3/4 c freshly grated
   Romano cheese
2 slices swiss cheese
   cut in strips

(see Veal Bolognese page 51, or you can
   use any good meatless spaghetti sauce)

Add garlic to oil and set aside. Pare the
eggplant, cut in ½ inch slices, sprinkle
liberally with salt and let stand ½ hour.
(I put it in a colander over a plate.)
Pat eggplant dry with paper towels, brush
with oil and lay on foil-lined baking pan.
Broil until lightly browned. (Watch! It
cooks quickly.) Brush once with oil if it
looks dry. Turn, brush with oil and brown
other side. Put several spoonfuls of the
sauce in a casserole, make a layer of the
eggplant, mask with sauce, sprinkle
with cheese — continue — ending with
sauce and cheese. Lay swiss cheese on
top. Bake at 350° 30-35 minutes. This
serves 2 as a main course, 4 as a vegetable.

We like this with green noodles or fettucini.

When the eggplants in the garden really
start producing, I do a four to six
eggplant version of this and freeze
it for the winter.

84

Eggplant *Farcie

1 unpeeled eggplant	1 t salt
3 T oil divided	1/2 t basil
1½ c cooked rice	1 t parsley minced
1 small onion chopped	1 c tomato sauce
1 green pepper diced	½ c crumbled
1 tomato, peeled, seeded	stuffing mix
and chopped	½ c grated sharp
1 C cooked corn	cheese

Cut eggplant in half lengthwise. Score the cut side ½ inch deep. Sprinkle with salt, lay cut side down and let stand ½ hour. Brown onion and green pepper lightly in 1 T oil. Add tomato and cook stirring until liquid evaporates. Turn into a large bowl and add rice, corn, salt, and herbs. Drain eggplant and pat dry. Brown cut side down in remaining 2 T oil for about 5 minutes. With a spoon, carefully remove pulp, leaving a ½ inch shell. Dice the pulp and add to rice mixture. Add ¾ of the tomato sauce, mix, and taste for seasoning, it may need more.

Put eggplant halves in a shallow baking pan. Spoon rice mixture into shells and mound. Drizzle with remaining tomato sauce. Sprinkle with stuffing mix and cheese. Bake at 375° for 45 minutes.   Serves 4.

*
When the zucchini in the garden get ahead of us, I do the same thing with them.

Spinach Timbales

Put everything into a blender container otherwise just combine all of the ingredients.

1 c cooked frozen chopped spinach
1 T butter
1 egg slightly beaten
½ c milk
¼ t fresh ground pepper

¼ t salt
few drops onion juice (or finely minced onion)
1 t mild vinegar
¼ t nutmeg

Blend well until smooth and put in buttered custard cups or timbale molds. Set in a pan of hot water and bake at 300° until firm when tried with a silver knife — about 40 minutes.

This amount makes 4.

We like these turned out onto a tomato slice on a slice of lightly toasted bread with a cheese sauce. I usually include them when, in summer, my husband asks for "just vegetables tonight." Really good with corn on the cob and a salad. Add a strip or two of bacon if you want to gild the lily.

Cider Mill Corn Pudding

Sweet corn is the one thing I haven't
room for in the garden, but with the Cider
Mill stand just down the road we have a
constant source of supply. Corn on the
cob never palls, but for an occasional
change, this is nice.

1 T oil	2 beaten eggs
½ green pepper diced	2 C milk
1 small onion diced	1 t season salt
2 C corn cut from cob	½ t pepper
(I use frozen in winter)	¼ t marjoram
½ C soft bread crumbs	½ C buttered crumbs

Lightly brown the green pepper and
onion in the oil. Add all of the other
ingredients except the buttered crumbs.
Mix and pour in a greased casserole.
Top with buttered crumbs. Set in a pan
of hot water and bake at 350° for 45
minutes or until a knife inserted in the
center comes out clean.   Serves 4.

This makes a nice meal with broiled
tomatoes, a green salad and a hot
bread.

Grilled Cheddar Cheese Sandwich

This is a favorite for luncheon when we have a guest or two, particularly with cream of leek or watercress soup. You can mix the filling ahead.

1½ c grated cheddar
4 t finely chopped green
   pepper
1 t worcestershire
½ t dry mustard
¼ t grated onion
4 slices rye bread
4 slices tomato
bacon or ham slices
   cooked (optional)

Gently toss cheese, green pepper, onion, worcestershire, and mustard, mixing well. Toast bread on one side only and butter lightly. Put two of the slices on a broiler pan, toasted side down. Arrange tomato slices on untoasted side and mound cheese on tomato. Run under broiler, six inches from heat until cheese melts and browns slightly. Put ham or bacon on top and cover with second toasted slice of rye. These can also be served open-faced.

Serves 2.

Vegetables

and Salads

"Let onion atoms dwell
within the bowl, and,
scarce suspected, animate
the whole."

Sydney Smith

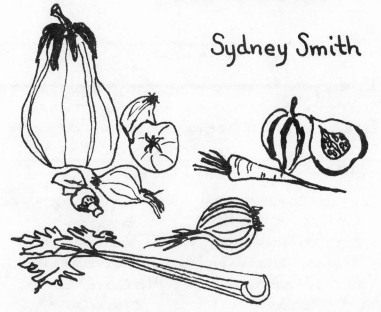

Shredded Zucchini

4 medium sized zucchini
  scrub well but do <u>not</u> pare
1 small onion chopped
1 T oil

½ t salt
¼ t pepper
1 bay leaf
1 T parsley

Lightly brown the onion in the oil.
Shred the zucchini on a grater using
the coarsest side. Add to the onion
in the pan. Stir to mix in onion and
coat with oil — add salt, pepper and
bay leaf. Cover tightly, turn heat down
and simmer 6-8 minutes. Stir once
or twice. Add a teaspoon of water
if it starts to stick. Serve
sprinkled with parsley. Serves 4.

Baked Onions in Sherry Sauce

I happen to be one of the people who
just loves creamed onions. These
are extra special — and - dear to
my heart — you can fix them
ahead.

2 · 1 lb. cans small
  white onions
1 c rich milk (or
  light cream)
⅓ c sherry
½ t salt

¼ t fresh ground
  pepper
3 T butter or
  margarine
⅓ c grated
  cheddar

Drain onions, rinse well under cold running water and drain again. Combine milk, sherry, salt and pepper, pour over onions in a shallow baking dish. Dot with butter. Sprinkle with cheese. Cover and bake at 350° for 20 minutes.

I've been told this serves 6 - but if you like them as I do - say 4.

Thyme Baked Carrots

6-8 carrots (it depends on the size)	1/4 t fresh ground pepper
1/2 t salt	1/2 t butter or margarine
1/4 t leaf thyme	2 T water

Pare carrots and slice, either straight across or, as I prefer, on the diagonal. Layer into a buttered casserole. Sprinkle each layer with salt, pepper, and just a hint of thyme, and dot with some of the butter. Add the water and bake, tightly covered, at 350° for 1 hour (375° for 45 minutes).   Serves 4.

Especially good with baked potatoes and maybe meat loaf or a baked fish.

Dividend Celery

4 C chopped leafy tops   ½ c water or
    from a large bunch   chicken broth
    of celery   ¼ t salt
2 T butter or margarine ⅛ t tarragon

Wash celery well, combine with the other
ingredients in a saucepan with a tight lid.
Cook, covered, about 8 minutes, or until
leaves wilt.   Serves 4.

A nice change from green little peas.

Michaelmas Broccoli and Cheese Casserole

We celebrated Michaelmas with friends and
this was part of our harvest celebration
feast.

2 packages frozen   ¼ t rosemary
   chopped broccoli   ¼ lb. mushrooms
1½ c grated sharp   sliced
   cheddar divided   1 small onion chopped
1 10 oz. can cream of   1 t oil
   mushroom soup   1 C crumbled dry
2 T sherry   stuffing mix
¼ t salt

92

Cook broccoli just enough to separate and drain well. Lightly brown mushrooms and onion in a large heavy saucepan. Stir in broccoli, 1 c cheese, soup, sherry, salt, and rosemary. Stir well and let the cheese melt. Pour in a greased casserole, sprinkle with stuffing mix, and top with remaining cheese. Bake at 350° for 30 minutes.   Serves 8.

Sherried Acorn Squash

These are often a part of Thanksgiving dinner.

2 acorn squash halved and seeded	grated rind of one orange
2 T butter or margarine	1/4 c dry sherry
3 T brown sugar	salt and pepper

Bake squash cut side down in a greased pan 40 minutes at 350°. Turn, brush with butter, sprinkle with sugar, orange peel, sherry, salt and pepper. Bake 20 minutes more.   Serves 4.

Sometimes I fix them ahead except for the last 20 minutes baking.

Skillet Carrots

I never really liked cooked carrots before
I tried them this way.

1 scant T butter or margarine	4 large carrots grated coarsely
a pinch of thyme	parsley
1/4 t salt	

In a skillet with a lid, melt the butter,
add thyme and salt — then grated
carrots. Toss to coat carrots with
butter. Cover and cook 5-8 minutes or
until well heated and tender but still
slightly crisp. Add 1t water if needed.
Sprinkle with parsley before serving.

Serves 4.

Herbed Potatoes

This is a good and unusual accompaniment
to a roast. A hearty addition to any
meal — leftovers make beautiful hashed
browned potatoes.

4 medium potatoes	fresh ground pepper
1/3 c flour	1 clove garlic minced
1/4 t thyme	1 bay leaf
1/2 t marjoram	3 T butter or margarine
3/4 t salt	

Butter a casserole. Peel and quarter the potatoes. Mix flour, herbs, salt and pepper. Dip the potatoes in the mixture and place in casserole. Toss in garlic and bay leaf. Dot with butter. Cover tightly and bake 40 minutes at 450°.

Serves 4.

Rice Salad

2 c cooked rice (either white or brown)	1/2 t salt
	1/4 t fresh ground pepper
1/2 c thinly sliced celery	1/4 t basil
1/2 green pepper chopped	1/4 c or more oil and vinegar dressing
1 carrot chopped	chopped parsley

Toss all of the ingredients but the parsley with the dressing and chill several hours. Serve on salad greens sprinkled with parsley.

Serves 6.

A nice change from potato salad.

Salade Provençal

I think you realize by now the manner in which we prefer to entertain. This salad is a blessing, particularly for a large dinner party—and the mixing method an innovation.

1 large or 2 small
   heads lettuce
1 bunch watercress
1 10 oz. package fresh
   spinach
2 jars marinated
   artichoke hearts
1 8 oz. can pitted
   ripe olives
1 bottle herb salad dressing

The night before or early in the day, wash and core the lettuce, then clean spinach and watercress under running water. Dry well. Remove spinach stems. Break up greens. Divide in two large plastic bags in refrigerator. Slice artichoke hearts and put back in marinade. Drain and halve olives. At serving time add one half of the olives and one jar of artichoke hearts with their marinade to the greens in each bag. Pour in one half of the dressing. Close bags tightly and shake to coat greens well. Pour into a large salad bowl.   Serves 12.

Shell Macaroni and Kidney Bean Salad

½ lb. small shell macaroni
   cooked and drained
1 16oz. can red kidney
   beans drained and
   rinsed
½ c pickle relish
4 hard-boiled eggs

1 small green pepper
   diced
¼ c french dressing
½ t basil
1 t salt
½ c mayonnaise
Salad greens

Toss shells, beans and relish with french dressing. Add the rest of the ingredients and mix lightly. Chill and serve on salad greens.
                    Serves 8.

My Salad Dressing*

⅓ c olive oil
⅓ c pure vegetable oil
⅓ c wine vinegar
1 t salt

¼ t paprika
¼ t fresh ground
   pepper
¼ t sugar
1 clove garlic halved

Combine all ingredients in a pint jar with a screw top. Shake well to blend. Makes 1 cup.

* For a creamy dressing, add 1 egg and beat well. Be sure you refrigerate this.

Jan's French Potato Salad

There is no worry about potato salad and hot weather when you do it this way.

4 medium potatoes
   unpeeled
1 onion chopped
1 t salt
½ t basil divided
¼ c dry white wine
2 stalks celery diced
½ green pepper diced
⅓ c oil and vinegar
   dressing divided
Sliced radishes
   parsley

Cook the potatoes with 1 t of the chopped onion, 1 t salt and ¼ t basil. Drain. While still hot, peel and slice. Pour on the white wine. Add remaining onion, basil, celery and green pepper. Pour ¼ c dressing on and toss lightly. Taste for seasoning, it may need more salt and basil. Just before serving, add remaining dressing and sprinkle with the radishes and chopped parsley. Serve warm or chilled.
                              Serves 4-6.

Breads

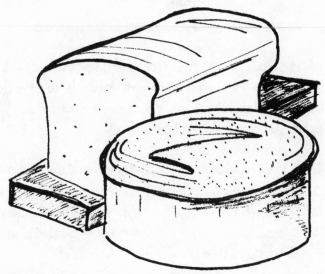

"Eat thy bread
with joy,
and drink thy wine
with a merry heart."

Ecclesiastes

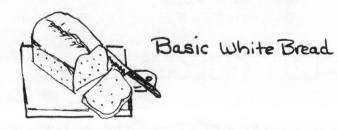

Basic White Bread

A good rule to remember when baking bread is to use a light hand with flour. Use a scant cup rather than a full one for a lighter loaf.

2 c hot water
2 T margarine or oil
2 T sugar
2 t salt
2/3 c dry skim milk

1 yeast cake dissolved in 1/4 c warm water
1/4 c wheat germ
6 - 6 1/4 c unbleached flour

Pour hot water into a large bowl, add margarine, sugar, salt, dry milk and yeast. Stir in the wheat germ and 3 C flour. Beat hard (at least 2-3 minutes). Add 2 c flour, mixing in with a knife. Add remaining flour gradually, using just enough to keep dough from being sticky. Turn out onto a floured board.

Knead 10 minutes until dough feels smooth and elastic. Put in a greased bowl, turn over to grease top. Cover and let rise until doubled (about 1 hour). Punch down, knead for a minute or two and form into two loaves. Place in greased loaf pans.

Cover and let rise until dough reaches top of pans.* Preheat oven to 400°, put in bread and immediately turn down to 375° Bake 40-45 minutes. Loaves should be well browned and sound hollow when tapped. Remove from pans. Cool on rack. For a soft crust, brush with melted butter.

*I find the top of a washer or dryer in use an ideal spot.

Variations:

1. Before forming loaves, knead ½c raisins into half of dough. Spread and stretch dough flat, sprinkle with 2T sugar mixed with 1t cinnamon. Roll up and tuck ends under to form loaf. (Use other loaf plain.)

2. For herb bread: add 2t crumbled sage, ½t nutmeg and 1t caraway seed when mixing dough.

3. For whole grain breads, replace not more than one half (3C) of flour with whole grain flours:

a. substitute ¼c wheat germ and 1¾c whole wheat flour for 2C unbleached flour. Substitute 2T brown sugar for 2T white sugar. Sprinkle unbaked loaves with sesame or poppy seeds.

b. Substitute 1 c oatmeal for 1 c unbleached flour and 2 T honey or maple syrup for 2 T sugar

c. Substitute 1 c rye flour, 1 c oatmeal and 1 c whole wheat flour for 3 c unbleached flour. Substitute 2 T molasses for 2 T sugar.

d. I often use 1 c leftover cereals or cooked rice or cracked wheat for part of the flour.

Nana's Oatmeal Bread

3 c sifted flour	1 egg
1 1/4 c quick oats (not instant)	1/4 c honey
	1 1/2 c milk
1 1/2 T baking powder	1/2 c raisins if
2 t salt	desired
	1 T butter or margarine

In a large bowl, mix flour, oats, baking powder and salt. In a medium bowl, beat egg with honey and milk. Pour egg mixture into oat mixture. Stir with a wooden spoon until dry ingredients are moistened. It will not be smooth. Add raisins if desired. Turn into a greased loaf pan. Bake at 350° for 1 hour and 15 minutes. Brush with melted butter. Cool on wire rack.

German Rye Bread

3 C unbleached flour
2 yeast cakes softened
  in 1/4 c warm water
1/4 c unsweetened cocoa
1 T caraway seed
1 3/4 c water
1/3 c molasses
2 T margarine
1 T sugar
2 t salt
3 - 3 1/2 c rye flour

In a large mixer bowl combine flour, cocoa and caraway seed until well blended. In a saucepan combine water, molasses, margarine, sugar and salt. Heat until margarine is melted, stirring occasionally. Add molasses mixture and yeast to dry mixture. Beat with electric mixer 1/2 minute, scrape bowl, beat 3 minutes at high speed. Stir in rye flour to make a soft dough. Turn out onto floured board and knead 10 minutes. Cover, let rest 20 minutes. Punch down — divide in half and make two round loaves. Put into two greased 8 inch pans. Brush with a little oil. Let rise until doubled (about an hour). Slash top three times. Bake at 400° about 30 minutes. Turn out. Cool on wire racks.

Baking Powder Biscuit Mix

I generally have several cupfuls of my own biscuit mix in the refrigerator. I find it just as easy to double this recipe and use it a cup at a time.

2 c flour
3 t baking powder
3/4 t salt
5 T shortening
    divided

Sift the dry ingredients together into a bowl. Add 3 T of the shortening and cut in until the mixture is in fine grains, then cut in remaining shortening. Store, tightly covered, in the refrigerator.

This makes 2 c mix.

Baking Powder Biscuits

2 c biscuit mix
2/3 - 3/4 c milk

Add milk to biscuit mix and stir in lightly with a fork. You may roll them out and cut with a biscuit cutter if you wish, but I always drop them by spoonfuls onto an ungreased baking sheet. Bake at 425° for 12-15 minutes.

Makes 8-12 biscuits.

Simple Irish Bread

Lovely for tea on a cold day — or for a
special breakfast.

2 c biscuit mix	½ c raisins
1 T shortening	1 T caraway seeds
½ c currants	⅔ c milk

Add the shortening to the biscuit mix
and cut in. Add fruit and caraway seeds
Stir in milk — if it looks dry — add a bit
more — it should have the consistency
of drop biscuits. Turn into a greased
8 inch skillet (with an oven-proof handle)
and bake at 350° for 25 minutes. Turn
up heat to 450° and bake 5 minutes
more. Serve warm in wedges.

Crust for Chicken or Meat Pie

You can heat the meat mixture in
the oven while making your crust.
Use the biscuit mix — but add to it a
good pinch of marjoram for chicken pie —
add basil for beef pie.

Drop by tablespoonfuls around the
edge of the pie and bake in a
450° oven 15 - 20 minutes until
browned.

Breadwinner

A recent winner in a "favorite recipe" contest. I was so excited when the judges called my name.

1 yeast cake
½ c warm water
⅛ t ginger
3 T sugar divided
1 13 oz. can evaporated milk
1 t salt
2 T salad oil
2 t celery seed
1½ t rubbed sage
⅛ t marjoram
½ c yellow cornmeal
4 c unsifted flour

Dissolve yeast in warm water in a large mixer bowl. Add ginger and 1 T sugar and blend well. Let stand until bubbly, about 20 minutes. Stir in the remaining sugar, the milk, salt, salad oil, celery seed, herbs and cornmeal. With mixer at low speed, beat in 2 c of flour, one at a time, beating well after each addition. Beat in last 2 c of flour with a wooden spoon. Add flour until dough is very heavy and stiff but too sticky to knead. Divide dough into 2 heavily greased 1 lb. coffee tins. Cover with well-greased plastic lids.

This bread "tells" you when it is ready to be baked. Let covered cans stand in a warm place until dough rises and pops off the lids (about 1 hour). Remove lids and bake at 350° 45 minutes (crust will be very brown). Brush top with melted butter. Let loaf stand in can 5-10 minutes before removing to wire rack to cool.

"Back of the loaf is the snowy flour,
   And back of the flour, the mill,
   and back of the mill is the wheat
   and the shower,
   And the sun and the Father's will."
                                    Babcock

Casserole Cheese Bread

This is a yeast <u>batter</u> bread — and a good and satisfying way to start making bread. I personally find bread-making a very rewarding job — and highly recommend the therapeutic effects of kneading. There was a time when my husband would say, "Why don't you get mad so we can have homemade bread?" Now I make it every week — you figure out what that says about my temper!

1 c milk	2 pkg. dry yeast
3 T sugar	1 c grated cheddar
1 T salt	4 1/2 c sifted flour
1 T margarine	1 t dry mustard
1 c very warm water	dash cayenne

Scald milk (or use 1/2 c evaporated milk and 1/2 c hot water); stir in sugar, salt and margarine. Cool to lukewarm. In a large mixing bowl, sprinkle yeast into very warm water. Stir until dissolved. Add milk mixture, cheese, flour, mustard and cayenne. Stir until well blended, about 2 minutes. Let rise in warm place until more than doubled in bulk, about 45 minutes. Stir down and beat hard 1/2 minute. Turn into greased 1 1/2 quart casserole and bake uncovered at 375° about 1 hour. Let stand 5-10 minutes before turning out onto wire rack to cool.

Plain Muffins et al.

I try to keep some in the freezer for our spur-of-the-moment breakfast picnics. By the time we get to our favorite spot by the river, they have thawed enough to heat quickly on the back of the camp stove while the coffee drips

2 C flour less 2T
3 t baking powder   1 c milk
½ t salt   3 ½ T oil
2 T sugar   1 egg beaten lightly

Mix and sift dry ingredients into bowl.* Beat egg in another bowl, add milk and oil. Add to flour mixture all at once. Stir just to dampen flour. Fill buttered muffin pans 2/3 full. Bake 15 minutes** at 400°.   Makes about 12.

<u>Blueberry</u>*- Reserve ¼ c flour. Sprinkle it over 1 c berries. Stir into batter last.
<u>Cranberry</u> - Mix an additional 2T sugar with 1 C cut cranberries and 1 t grated orange rind. Decrease milk to ½ c and add ½ c orange juice.
<u>Orange-Date</u> - Add 1 ½ t orange rind, ½ c chopped dates. Use ½ c milk and ½ c orange juice. Sprinkle tops with sugar.

**I find all of the fruit muffins take at least 10-15 minutes longer to bake.

Crêpes

I usually make a double batch of these and when they are cooled, stack them separated with plastic film, and freeze, wrapped in foil. They thaw almost instantly in a colander over boiling water for a glamorous breakfast or brunch — or can be filled with almost anything for a quick dinner or dessert. Versatile to say the least.

1 c cold water	½ t salt
1 c cold milk	2 c sifted flour
4 eggs	4 T melted butter

Put water, milk, eggs and salt in blender container, then add flour and butter. Cover, blend 1 minute. Scrape sides with rubber spatula and blend 2-3 seconds longer. Cover and refrigerate at least 2 hours. (I have found if you use instant type flour you can cook them immediately.) Brush a 6½-7 inch skillet with oil. Heat until it begins to smoke. Remove from heat, ladle ¼ c of batter into pan. Tilt pan to cover bottom with a thin film. Return pan to heat 60 to 80 seconds. Shake pan to loosen crêpe. When light brown on bottom, turn (I use my fingers but you can use a fork or spatula). Brown lightly (½ minute) on other side. Turn out onto paper towels if you are making them to use later, or keep warm in a low oven. Oil pan for each crêpe. This makes 12-16 6-6½ inch crêpes.

To reheat for breakfast crêpes: thaw— fold in quarters and heat in a little butter. Serve with jam or syrup.

For dinner we especially like them filled with chicken or salmon and mushrooms in a rich cream or velouté sauce (see page 60) and rolled up. Spoon an additional tablespoon or two of sauce over them, and top with grated Swiss cheese. Bake at 350° for 20-25 minutes.

Ham and broccoli or asparagus with a cheese sauce is also nice.

For dessert crêpes, fold in quarters and heat in a little butter. We like them with this sauce:

1 c tawny port
¼ c brown sugar
½ t grated lemon rind
½ t lemon juice
1 c blueberries

Combine wine, sugar and rind in a saucepan. Heat, stirring until sugar dissolves and liquid begins to bubble. Add berries and heat through. Ladle warm sauce over crêpes. Serves 4.

Sue's Christmas Bread

This was included in a friend's Christmas card a few years ago and has become a part of our holidays.

1 egg slightly beaten
½ c butter or margarine
½ c milk
1 yeast cake
½ c warm water
¼ c sugar
1 t salt
1 c raisins

½ c candied fruit (pour boiling water over, drain and dice)
½ c sliced almonds
3½-4 c sifted flour
¼ c confectioner's sugar

Reserve 1T beaten egg. Heat butter and milk, cool to lukewarm. Soften yeast in warm water, stir in sugar, salt, raisins, fruit, nuts, remaining egg and milk mixture. Add flour gradually to make a stiff dough. Knead 10 minutes. Let rise in a warm place until doubled (about 2 hours). Shape into 2 round loaves, place in greased 8 inch pans. Cover, let rise until doubled (about 1 hour). Bake at 350° 30-35 minutes. Brush with reserved egg. When cool sprinkle with confectioner's sugar. (I put it in a small strainer and sift it on.)

Desserts

"'Tis the dessert
that graces all the feast,
for an ill end
disparages all the rest."

William King

Piecrust

This makes a 9-10 inch double crust. I find that if the unbaked crust is stored a day or two (or even a week) in the refrigerator it is much improved.

2¼ c sifted flour ⎤ Sift this into a medium
1 t salt   ⎬   sized bowl
small pinch nutmeg⎦
¾ c shortening —— Add half of shortening and cut in until fine as Indian meal. Cut in rest of shortening until size of navy beans.
5 T cold water (or less)

Sprinkle water gradually over mix. Work with a fork until moistened and in small lumps. Put dampened particles together into a ball (when I have time I chill it here.) Roll out half at a time. Bake as per recipe.

If your recipe calls for 1 baked shell, use half recipe or make two crusts and refrigerate one for later use. In this case, prick well all over crust. Bake at 425° for 12-15 minutes.

Brown Bag Apple Pie

1 unbaked 9 inch pie shell
3-4 baking apples (2½ lbs.)
½ c sugar
2 T flour
½ t nutmeg
¼ t salt
2 T lemon juice

For topping:
½ c sugar
½ c flour
½ c butter or
margarine

Pare, core and quarter apples, then cut each quarter crosswise to make chunks (you should have about 7 cups) and put in large bowl. Combine sugar, flour, salt and nutmeg, sprinkle over apples and toss to coat well. Put in pie shell and drizzle with lemon juice.

Combine sugar and flour for topping and cut in butter. Sprinkle over apples to cover top.

Slide pie into heavy brown paper bag large enough to cover pie loosely, fold open end over twice and fasten with paper clips. Place on a cookie sheet for easy handling.

Bake at 425° 1 hour (apples will be tender and top bubbling and golden). Split bag open, remove pie and cool on a rack. Serve warm. Good with a sharp cheese.

Vermont Pumpkin Pie

If an excuse is needed to justify a trip to Vermont, maple syrup will do nicely. Since it both cans and freezes easily, keeping it is no problem. This is one of my favorite cooking uses.

2 c strained pumpkin
1 c maple syrup
3 eggs – reserve one white
1 t (or more) salt
3/4 t ginger

1 1/4 t cinnamon
1/2 t nutmeg
1 3/4 c evaporated milk
1 unbaked 10 inch pie shell, chilled

Mix pumpkin, syrup, 2 whole eggs and 1 egg yolk, salt and spices. Add milk gradually. Mix well. I try to do this several hours before I bake it so flavors can blend. Just before baking, stir well, then whip reserved egg white stiff. Fold into pumpkin mixture, and pour into unbaked pie shell. Bake at 450° 10 minutes, turn heat down to 350° and bake 30 minutes more, or until a knife inserted in center comes out clean.

Plumb Good Cobbler

Filling:
1 lb. 14 oz. can purple
   plums
1/4 c orange juice
2 T sugar
1 T cornstarch
1/2 t cinnamon

Topping:
1 1/2 c biscuit mix
   (see page 104)
1/2 c milk
2 T melted butter
   or margarine
2 T brown sugar

Drain and pit plums, reserving syrup, and put them in a 6 cup baking dish. Stir syrup and orange juice into a mixture of the sugar, cornstarch and cinnamon in a small pan. Cook, stirring, over medium heat until sauce thickens and boils one minute. Pour the sauce over the plums and heat in a 400° oven until bubbling while making topping.

Blend biscuit mix and milk and spoon the dough in 6 mounds on top of hot fruit. Drizzle mixture of butter and brown sugar over biscuits.

Bake at 400° for 15 minutes. Serve warm, with cream if you like, to 6.

A good fall or winter dessert.

Sherry Walnut Pie

¼ c butter
2 T flour
½ c dark corn syrup
⅓ c medium sherry
1 c sugar

3 eggs lightly beaten
1 c coarsely broken
  walnuts
1 unbaked 9 inch
  pie shell

Melt butter. Stir in flour, then syrup, wine and sugar. Cook over moderate heat — stirring constantly until thickened and smooth. Gradually stir the hot mixture into the eggs. Add nuts and pour into pie shell. Bake 45 minutes at 375° — or until firm. Cool before serving.

This is something different and, we think, a nice change from Pecan Pie.

Orange Lemon Cake

I keep the ingredients for this cake on my emergency shelf — it is even better if made a day or two ahead, and it freezes well.

1 package yellow mix
1 package orange
  gelatin
¾ c water
¾ c oil
4 eggs

For glaze:
2 c confectioner's
  sugar
juice and rind of
  2 lemons

118

Ignore the package directions. Mix the cake ingredients together until smooth. Turn into a greased and floured 10 inch tube pan and bake at 350° for 45-55 minutes (a toothpick comes out clean). When cake is baked, but before it cools, set on a wire rack over a deep plate. Prick top of cake well with a long-tined fork and spoon over the lemon glaze until it is absorbed.

Orange Sponge Cups

2 T butter
⅔ c sugar
2 eggs separated

¼ c undiluted frozen orange juice concentrate
2 T flour
1 c milk

Cream butter and add sugar. Cream again. Add egg yolks and beat well. Add juice, then flour. Add milk, blending well (it will look curdled, but don't worry). Beat egg whites until stiff and fold into orange mixture. Pour into 4 or 5 greased custard cups. Put in a pan of hot water and bake 35 minutes at 350°. Chill and unmold.

This separates into a cake layer and a custard layer. I garnish it with fresh orange sections or canned mandarin oranges.

Nana Hoyt's Yum-yum Cake

A classic in the Hoyt-Brandon family—
an eggless, milkless, butterless "economy
cake"— this keeps very well (if you hide it).
For an easy fruitcake, add a cup of
mixed candied fruits and a cup of
walnuts or pecans.

Boil together for 5 minutes:
2 c sugar	2 t salt
2 c water	3 t cinnamon
2 T shortening	½ package
	muscat raisins

When **completely** **cold** add 3 c flour.
Dissolve 1 heaping t baking soda in a
little water. Mix into batter very well.
Turn into a well-greased and floured
9 inch tube pan (or a 9 inch square
pan). Bake in a 325° oven at least
45 minutes (it usually takes 60-65)
until a toothpick inserted in the
center comes out clean.

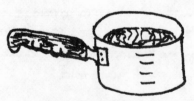

If I frost this at all (which I usually
don't), I use just confectioner's sugar
and water and a dusting of
nutmeg.

Cocoa Cake

I don't know why it works, but for an easy
to make cake try this.

1½ C sifted flour	⅓ c oil
1 C sugar	1 T vinegar
3 T unsweetened cocoa	1 t vanilla
1 t baking powder	1 C cold water
½ t salt	

Measure dry ingredients into sifter. Sift
together twice, the last time directly
into an ungreased 9 x 9 cake pan. Make
three depressions in dry ingredients. Pour
oil into one, vinegar into second, and
vanilla into third. Pour water over all.
Mix with fork until dry ingredients
disappear. The batter will be thin. Bake
at 350° for 40 minutes. <u>Do not</u> attempt to
turn out. Cool, ice and slice in pan.

This travels well for picnics.

Mama Bergeron's Bliss Cake

A favorite special occasion dessert in my husband's family.

For cake:
- ½ c vegetable shortening
- ½ c sugar
- 4 egg yolks
- 1 c cake flour
- 2 t baking powder
- ¼ t salt
- ⅓ c milk
- 1 t vanilla

For meringue:
- 4 egg whites
- 4 T sugar
- 1 t vanilla
- ½ c walnuts chopped

For filling:
- 1 c whipping cream
- 1 8oz. can crushed pineapple, drained

In a large bowl, cream the shortening and sugar together. Add egg yolks, one at a time, beating well after each. Sift the flour, baking powder and salt together twice. Add to creamed mixture alternately with milk. Add vanilla. Grease and flour two 9 inch round cake pans, spread in batter (it will look scant and runny). Beat egg whites stiff with sugar, add vanilla. Spread over batter in each pan and sprinkle with the nuts. Bake at 325° for 45 minutes. Remove from pans and cool on wire racks.

Beat the cream stiff and fold in pineapple. Put one cake layer, meringue side down, on serving plate, cover with cream mixture and set other layer on top — meringue side up. Chill well.
Serves 8-10.

Two-Tone Coffee Cream

A favorite summer dessert.

1 envelope plain gelatin	2 c milk heated to
1/2 c sugar divided	scalding
1/8 t salt	2 T instant coffee
2 eggs separated	1 t vanilla

Mix gelatin, 1/4 c sugar and salt in top of double boiler. Beat egg yolks, gradually add hot milk. Add instant coffee and stir into gelatin mixture. Cook over simmering water, stirring constantly, until gelatin is dissolved and mixture slightly thickened, (8-10 minutes). Remove from heat and add vanilla. Cool while you beat egg whites until stiff, gradually adding remaining sugar. Fold into custard mixture. Pour immediately into sherbet dishes. Let stand until it separates into 2 layers — then chill until set.
Serves 6.

Bittersweet Chocolate Pudding

This is the closest I could come to a dessert served at New York's "Top-of-the-Sixes". There they serve it with a lightly beaten whipped cream (the French call it Crème Chantilly) and a drizzle of Creme de cacao. We like it also with a __bit__ of vanilla ice cream to melt over it.

3 squares bitter chocolate   1/4 t salt
1 c milk   3 unbeaten eggs
1/2 c sugar   1 t vanilla
1/2 t cinnamon

In the top of a double boiler combine the chocolate, milk, sugar, cinnamon and salt. Heat over simmering water until chocolate is melted. Beat with a rotary beater until smooth. Add vanilla to eggs and add to chocolate mixture all at once. Beat 1 minute. Cover and cook over simmering water for 40 minutes. Serve hot to 4.

If you keep the water warm under the pudding after it has cooked it holds very well for an hour or more. Also it reheats the same double boiler way.

This __is__ __so__ __good__!

Mousse au Chocolat

A blender recipe that is so good and so easy it must be sinful!

1 6oz. package semi-sweet chocolate bits
5 T boiling water
4 egg yolks
2 T dark rum (for Mousse au Mocha use creme de café)
4 stiffly beaten egg whites

Put chocolate in blender container and blend 6 seconds. Scrape sides, add boiling water and blend 6 seconds again. Add egg yolks and rum and blend 3 seconds. <u>Stir</u> about one quarter of the egg whites into the chocolate mixture to lighten it (wish I had known that trick twenty years ago) then pour chocolate mixture over rest of egg whites and fold together, very gently until no streaks of white remain. Spoon into serving dishes. Chill overnight.   Serves 4-6.

Don't panic! It is fairly thin and it thickens as it chills. I say this because I nearly had a fit the first time I made it.

English Shortbread

A treasured recipe from an English friend— and always included in our Christmas cookies. A "good keeper."

2¼ c unsifted flour
6¾ T cornstarch
½ c sugar

½ c butter } cut in 1 inch pieces
½ c margarine)

Sift the dry ingredients together twice. Gently rub in the fats with your fingers to break up the pieces. Knead together with your knuckles until mixture adheres.

Line a 9x9 pan with wax paper. Grease and flour it. Press the mixture in firmly. Bake at 350° for 40-45 minutes until lightly brown. Cool slightly in pan — sprinkle with granulated sugar (I use red and green for the holidays), cut in strips. Take out carefully and put on rack to cool completely. Store airtight.

Lemon Squares

These are tart-sweet and rich enough to stand alone for dessert. For buffet parties I find a variety of cookies makes an excellent dessert.

For crust:
1 c flour
1/4 c confectioner's sugar
1/2 c butter or margarine

For topping:
2 eggs
1 C granulated sugar
1/2 t baking powder
1/4 t salt
grated rind and juice of 1 lemon

Sift flour and confectioner's sugar together, cream with butter. Press evenly into a 9x9 baking pan. Bake at 350° for 20 minutes.

While crust bakes, beat eggs and sugar until fluffy, add baking powder and salt and beat in. Then stir in rind and juice. Spoon evenly over baked crust and bake 25-30 minutes longer, until no imprint remains when touched lightly in center. Cool. Then cut in squares.   Makes about 24.

Cranberry Oaten Bars

You can serve these either as cookies, or warm them and put a scoop of vanilla ice cream on top. Good either way—and one of our favorites.

- 1 c quick oats
  (not instant)
- 1 c brown sugar
- ½ c flour
- ¼ lb. butter or margarine
- ¼ t salt
- 1 8oz. can whole berry
  cranberry sauce

Cream oats, sugar, flour, butter and salt together. Press half of this into bottom of a greased 9x9 baking pan. Spread cranberry sauce evenly over this and sprinkle with remaining oat mixture. Press gently into cranberry sauce to even top. Bake 45 minutes at 350°. Let sit a minute or two before cutting into bars and removing to cool on wire rack. (Dip knife in hot water, it helps.)

Makes 24.

Things I Wish I'd Known

"If thou of fortune be bereft
And in thy store there be but left
Two loaves—sell one, and with the dole
Buy hyacinths to feed thy soul."

Anon.

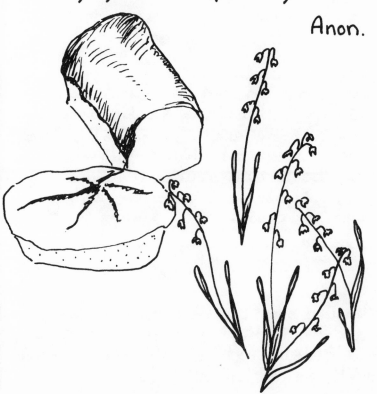

Cook with your nose! Should it smell so good so soon? When certain recipes say "Put in a 500° oven and lower the heat immediately to 350°", they really mean immediately.

Sniff the cream if it is supposed to be sweet, and the oil, and taste the nuts. Things do get stale or sour.

Hot things in the blender have a foaming, whooshing exuberance you wouldn't believe. Do not fill container more than one-third full — or you may be scraping cream sauce off your eyebrows and the ceiling. Let it cool!

Measure over the bare counter or the sink — not the bowl you are adding to. Elbows get joggled — things that stick come all at once.

When you cook eggs in the shell, put a
big teaspoon of salt in the water.
The shells won't crack.

Rubbing raw mushrooms with lemon
before adding them to a recipe keeps
them white and professional looking.

If when baking you add your flavoring
extract to the shortening while creaming,
it develops much more flavor.

When increasing a recipe, write it down
before you start. Use only half again
as much salt or spices and then
taste.

Undercook pasta and vegetables that
will be in a casserole — for frozen
vegetables this means just long enough
to separate — for most pasta - five
minutes.

If butter is hard to cream, slice it into a warmed bowl.

When something tastes not quite zingy enough, don't add salt — try a few drops of lemon juice. This is especially true with creamed dishes and fish.

DO NOT - DO NOT overcook fish! The devil with the times the cookbooks say! Start testing after about 3 (yes, that _is_ three) minutes for broiled fish — 6-8 minutes for baked fish. It is done as soon as it loses its translucence and becomes opaque. Twenty to thirty minutes — Nonsense!

While I am thinking of onions — put one in a small glass on the window-sill with about 1/8 inch water in the bottom of the glass — in a day or so you have lovely green onions — cut off what you need, more keep coming.

When stuffing a chicken or turkey—prop it in one corner of the sink with the bowl of stuffing on the counter just above —any spills go into the sink. Makes for an easy clean-up.

Forget the package directions for cooking frozen vegetables. Melt as much butter or margarine in a pan as you would normally use after they are cooked. You can brown a little onion or mushrooms in this if you want. Put in the solidly frozen vegetables, turn down heat and let them cook in the amazing amount of water in which they are frozen. Takes a bit longer — tastes a bit better.

I used to worry when a roast was done 15 to 20 minutes (or more) before anything else. then I found it is _supposed_ to rest. It is easier to carve and much more flavorful.

Never cook with a wine you would not drink.

If you put a healthy sprinkle of salt on the spot when red wine is spilled on a tablecloth — immediately — it will not stain.

When you pressure-cook meat or poultry, forget the directions to reduce the pressure slowly. Run pan under cold water, as for vegetables, to reduce pressure immediately, open, taste for seasoning, add a little wine and simmer 5-10 minutes. This gets rid of the "steamed" taste.

For some unknown reason, gelatin will not set properly in a plastic bowl.

For guests, prepare only those dishes you do most easily, no matter how simple, and concentrate on garnishing and a pretty table to provide a party look.

The difference between a good cook and a poor one is often only a tablespoon of butter.

You get better results when baking if you remember to preheat your pans while the oven heats.

A teaspoon of vanilla added to just about any cake mix makes the cake taste more homemade.

I wish I had known that anyone who can read can cook! Just follow directions — and add half an hour longer than you think you need.

Notes

Notes

Notes

Notes

Notes

Notes

Notes

Notes

Notes